St. J[...]

as Patron Saint

REV. JUDE WINKLER, OFM Conv.

Imprimi Potest: James McCurry, OFM Conv., Minister Provincial of St. Anthony of Padua Province (USA)
Nihil Obstat: Rev. Msgr. James M. Cafone, M.A., S.T.D., Censor Librorum
Imprimatur: ✠ **Most Rev. John J. Myers, D.D., J.C.D.**, Archbishop of Newark

The Nihil Obstat and Imprimatur are official declarations that a book or pamphlet is free of doctrinal or moral error. No implication is contained therein that those who have granted the Nihil Obstat and Imprimatur agree with the contents, opinions or statements expressed.

Printed in Hong Kong   ISBN 978-0-89942-543-6   CPSIA   November 2011   10 9 8 7 6 5 4 3 2   A/P

Foster Father of Jesus

WHEN God created Adam and Eve, He placed them in the Garden of Eden. He provided for them, giving them everything that they needed. But He told them not to eat the fruit of the tree of good and evil.

They disobeyed God and He punished them. Yet, He also promised them that He would send a Savior Who would free them and their children from their sins.

In time, God sent the Angel Gabriel to the Blessed Virgin Mary. He asked her to be the Mother of God's only Son. Mary, who was so good and generous, said, "Yes" to God's call.

God also sent a man to care for Mary and her Baby, Jesus. His name was Joseph. He was a carpenter and was engaged to Mary.

Joseph did not understand how Mary could be carrying a Baby and wanted to send her away. Yet, when an Angel from God appeared to him in a dream and told him to take care of Mary and her Child, he listened to the Angel.

Joseph, unlike Adam and Eve, obeyed God. He was filled with compassion and he took them into his home and his heart.

The Head of the Holy Family

GOD chose Joseph to be the head of the Holy Family. The Father knew that Joseph was a holy man. God blessed him with every grace to be a loving husband to Mary and a caring father to Jesus. His many good qualities would help him in the all-important role of leading the Holy Family.

First, Joseph was a man of faith. He believed in God and His plan for his own small family and the bigger plan for all of God's family. He and Mary showed their faith by obeying God, no matter what difficulties faced them. They shared their faith with their Son by respecting and observing its laws and traditions.

Joseph was caring and compassionate. He made sure that Mary was comfortable on the way to Bethlehem. Finding no housing when they arrived there, he searched until he could find a safe place where their Son could be born. He knew the importance of family.

Joseph worked hard to provide his family with basic needs like food and shelter. He was no doubt honest and fair and made items of good quality.

With Joseph as their head, his family lived a simple life, but one filled with peace and joy.

Protector of the Holy Family

THE Holy Family did not always have an easy life. They had to go through some difficulties. Joseph was always there to guide and protect them.

When Jesus was just a Baby, King Herod tried to hurt Him. Herod was afraid that this newborn King of the Jews would steal his throne. He therefore ordered his soldiers to go to Bethlehem and kill all of the baby boys there who were two years old and younger.

But God protected the Holy Family from his plans. He sent an Angel in a dream to warn the three Magi who visited Jesus not to go back to King Herod. That same Angel also told Joseph to take Mary and the Baby into Egypt where they would find safety.

It must have been hard to have to leave a place where they felt safe and travel to a distant land. But Joseph obeyed God's command because he trusted that God would protect them.

When King Herod died and the danger was over, an Angel appeared to Joseph again to tell him to go home.

Joseph, Mary, and Jesus traveled to the town of Nazareth where Joseph and Mary cared for Jesus as He grew up.

Protector of Families

JUST as Joseph protected the Holy Family, so he will watch over our families and help them to become more like his own family.

We have already seen how Joseph protected Jesus from King Herod.

Yet, once when they had been in Jerusalem for the Feast of Passover, Joseph lost track of Jesus. He and Mary thought He was with other travelers in their group, but He was not. Fearful for His safety, they returned to Jerusalem and found Him in the Temple with the teachers. Joseph and Mary acted quickly to bring their Son once again under their protection.

Besides being a model for keeping families safe, Joseph reminds us that our families should be generous and not think only of themselves. God calls us to share the blessings that He has given us with those who live with far less than we do.

He also provided a fine example to Jesus Who grew up to be good and generous. Jesus had the perfect models of generosity of heart in His Mother, Mary, and His foster father, Joseph.

When we read about the Holy Family and we reflect on their lives, we see an example of what our own families can become.

Protector of Children

GOD calls each of us to a different vocation. He gives us the talents that we need to do that work well.

This is certainly true of Joseph. He was called to be the foster father of Jesus. He protected Him from danger. Joseph showed his Son how to be a caring, loving, and generous man. He provided a living for the Holy Family. He even taught Jesus how to be a carpenter like he was.

Now that Joseph is in heaven, he continues to protect children. He intercedes for them with God, asking Him to keep them safe from all harm. He gives them the good example of humble, generous service. He teaches them that they should not be lazy, because in helping others, they are continuing the work of God here on earth. He and Mary also teach children how to pray and worship God, just as they taught Jesus to do.

Joseph guides children away from temptation. Sometimes they can be tempted to want their own way even if it hurts others. At other times, they also may not listen to their parents or be unkind to their brothers and sisters. It is at these times when children can look to Joseph. He will remind them to be generous, obedient, and calm, as Jesus had been growing up.

Model of Single and Married Men

IN the simple way he lived his life from day to day, Joseph was a wonderful example for all men. He focused on his faith, his family, and others.

Joseph strongly believed in his God and the faith shared by those who came before him. Without question, he trusted in God as he was told by Angels to take Mary as his wife, to flee to Egypt to protect Jesus from harm, and to return to Nazareth when the danger had passed. A prayerful man, Joseph made prayer a central part of his family life.

Joseph knew how important his family was. He loved Mary with a husband's love; he also respected her and was devoted to her. Joseph treasured his role as parent to Jesus. He loved Jesus as only a father could. He kept Him safe and showed Him how to make an honest living until He began His public ministry.

As a carpenter, Joseph was able to provide for his family. He made things that were necessary for people to have or that would help them to make their homes more comfortable. Even his work led him to focus on others' well being.

All men can be thankful to Joseph for showing them a clear way to lead their lives.

Guardian of Virgins

JOSEPH is often called the guardian of virgins, people who are chaste and pure.

Mary our Mother is well known as a virgin. She was a virgin before she gave birth to Jesus because she was with Child by the power of the Holy Spirit. She also remained a virgin after she gave birth to her Son. Perhaps Mary's greatest title is Blessed Virgin Mother.

Joseph, too, was a virgin. He and Mary respected one another and the role each played in God's plan. They remained devoted to one another and showed their love for one another throughout their marriage.

There have been many virgins among the Saints, like Catherine of Siena and Thérèse of the Child Jesus. These women made a special promise to God to remain pure and never to marry or have children. They chose instead to dedicate their lives to love of God and in service to His children.

Of course, there are virgins who are not Saints. They live their lives in harmony with God's desire for them to respect themselves, remaining pure until marriage.

It is Joseph to whom all can turn to guide and help them to live pure and modest lives.

Model of Righteousness

JOSEPH was a righteous man because he did what was fair and just and chose to follow God's ways.

It was important to him that he and Mary kept God's Commandments. He also made sure that they observed the traditions of their Jewish faith.

After forty days, the Holy Family went to the Temple in Jerusalem. The Jewish law required that new mothers had to be purified, and this ceremony took place forty days after the birth of her child.

Because Jesus was their firstborn, His parents had to offer a small sacrifice to buy Him back. This recalled how God had saved all the firstborn of the people of Israel from the Angel of death when He brought His people out of Egypt. From the little they had, Joseph and Mary offered two small birds.

Besides following the law, Joseph lived his life every day by being charitable, honest, and kind. He was a loving family man. His neighbors could count on him when they were in need. He treated everyone fairly.

Joseph will always show us the right way to act.

Patron of Priests and Seminarians

JOSEPH is also the Patron Saint of priests and seminarians, those who are studying to be priests. A Patron is a Saint who dedicates himself to the service of those who need his aid. Priests and seminarians often call upon Joseph for his heavenly help.

Why would Joseph be their Patron Saint? There are a number of reasons for this.

He was the head of the Holy Family, just as priests are called to lead those in their care. Like Joseph, they are to do this through humble, compassionate service.

Joseph and Mary protected Jesus and helped Him grow up so that He could preach God's Word to Israel. Priests protect the Church. They preach God's Word and celebrate the Sacraments to make Jesus present again to all of us.

Priests are called to be celibate (pure and unmarried) so that they might serve the Church in every part of their lives. Joseph is a model of this for he served the Holy Family in the same way.

Joseph is also a model of prayer and obedience to the call of God. Priests and seminarians are to be men of prayer, always ready to obey God's call wherever it might lead them.

Model of Christian Workers

JOSEPH knew the importance of work. He understood that by working, he could provide for the needs of his family: food, clothing, and a roof over their heads.

The town of Nazareth, where the Holy Family lived, was poor. Most people there wanted to own some land and be farmers. Joseph, however, was too poor to own land and therefore became a carpenter to support his family. He took pride in his work, making wooden objects that could be used by his neighbors in their homes. Joseph taught Jesus to be a carpenter, too, so that He could make a living.

Joseph is a perfect example for workers today. He used a talent that God gave him. In doing so, he not only provided for his family but also served those who needed what he made.

Although what he did was seen by most people as lowly, he was proud of his work and worked hard. He was honest and fair with everyone.

Work is a fact of life. It may not always be easy. With Joseph as our guide, however, we can better appreciate it as something that we are called to do by God to serve Him and others.

Consoler of the Poor

POVERTY was something Joseph knew very well. He and his family experienced it themselves throughout their lives. When Jesus was born, He was surrounded by animals that were kept in the cave Joseph found for his family to stay.

The offering that Joseph and Mary made when they presented Jesus in the Temple forty days after He was born was two small birds. This was what was given by those who were poor.

Joseph did not have enough money to own land so he could raise crops for his family. Owning land was viewed by people in his time as a sign of success. He instead became a carpenter, something seen as lowly work in his day. Because the Holy Family lived in Nazareth, a very poor place, it is thought that their home there was a cave.

Joseph can understand exactly what it means to be poor. He knows the difficulties of providing for a family and keeping them safe. He knows what it is like not to have the best housing. He knows how things can be when a low-paying job is the only one to be found. Therefore, he is perhaps the best person to look to for hope and guidance when facing such difficult times.

Rescuer of Sinners

FROM all we know about Joseph, he was a good and holy man. He knew right from wrong and chose to do the Will of God and obey His Commandments.

Because of his goodness and compassion, it seems that he is a natural choice for sinners to turn to for understanding. With his quiet and gentle way, Joseph appears to listen without judging people for their mistakes. He simply wants to guide them to a better way of living.

Sometimes people just need to know that others are not against them because they have done wrong. They may not know how to turn away from their sinful actions without a caring hand to help them. Joseph has a concern for all God's children and wants to lend a helping hand.

Joseph understands how deep God's love is for all people. He knows that God created people to be good and to do what is good. He has faith that the Father's forgiveness is waiting for those who seek it.

With his loving and caring ways, Joseph is a perfect person to remind sinners that if they turn away from sin and toward God, forgiveness is theirs.

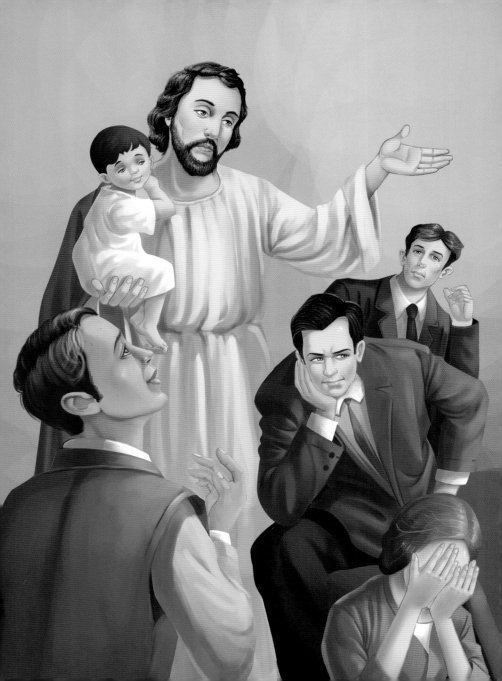

Comfort to the Afflicted

SOMETIMES life does not go the way we hope. Even if we are faithful to God, at some point troubles will enter our lives. Joseph understands, and he provides hope and comfort to people when they are hurting.

Joseph faced the difficult and unexpected during his life. When he and Mary were engaged, Joseph probably thought that their life together would be quiet and happy. Yet, their lives changed forever once the Angel Gabriel appeared to Mary and asked her to be the Mother of God's Son.

After a tiring trip to Bethlehem, Mary and Joseph could find no room where they could stay. Their Child had to be born among animals in a cave because it was the only place where they could find shelter.

Joseph and Mary faced the pain of not knowing where their Son was for several days after a trip to Jerusalem for the Feast of Passover.

Yet, when something bad happened, Joseph and Mary saw in it a way to follow God's Will. They were not sure how things would turn out well, but they trusted that God would make all things right for them. The example of Joseph and Mary comfort us as we deal with the difficulties that come our way.

Hope of the Sick

WHEN we are sick, we often wonder whether God has left us. When those we love are sick, it breaks our heart. We hate to see them hurting so badly. We even tell God that we would rather suffer than to watch them suffer.

Joseph is a source of hope for us when we or those we love are sick. He intercedes with God on our behalf, and people often have been healed through a miracle of God's love.

Compassionate Joseph reminds us to trust in God's care. He places himself alongside of us as we lie in bed so that we will never have to suffer alone. His presence is a sign of God's love for us.

He helps us remember that each of us is called to carry our cross with love. We can offer up our suffering and make it into an act of love. We can tell God that we wish to join our suffering to that of another who is suffering more than we are. By doing this, we make sure that someone else does not have to suffer alone. We also make another's cross just a bit lighter to carry.

We can join our sufferings to those of Jesus and be willing to carry our cross just as He did. By doing this, God's love might shine through us.

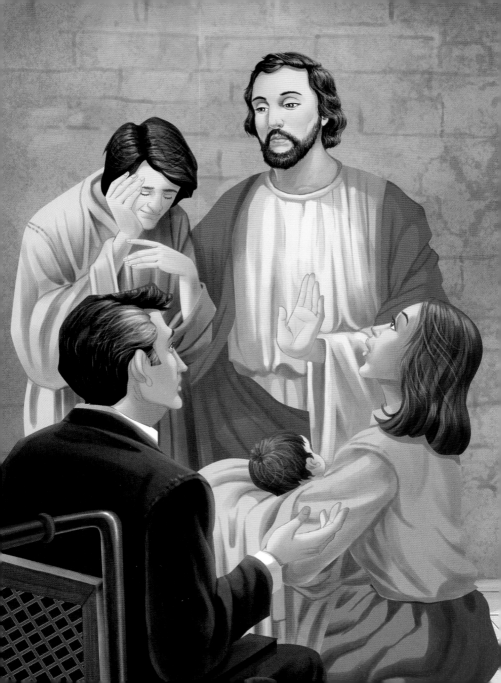

Patron of a Happy Death

OF all the people who ever died, Joseph must have had one of the holiest deaths. We do not know exactly when he died, but we do know who was there with him. Jesus and the Blessed Virgin Mary were alongside of him, holding his hand and reminding him to trust in God.

What a comfort! By his side was Mary who had given her life and love to God when she agreed to be the Mother of Jesus. Joseph had cared for her for so many years, and now she was caring for him.

Beside him, too, was Jesus. He was Joseph's adopted Son, but He also was his Savior. With Him at his side, he no longer needed to fear death. It was not something to worry about anymore. In fact, it was the doorway to heaven.

Joseph now does for us what Mary and Jesus did for him. He is inside us as we prepare for our own deaths.

Like Mary, he reminds us to say our "Yes" to God's plan. He also reminds us that because of Jesus' death on the Cross, death is no more. It cannot defeat us because Jesus has defeated it.

Death for us, like it was for Joseph, is now our doorway to heaven.

Patron of
the Universal Church

IN 1870, Pope Pius the Ninth declared that St. Joseph is the Patron for the whole Church. We call upon him to protect the Church today, even as he protected the Holy Family, which was the first true Christian Church.

Pray this prayer to ask for his help:

Dear St. Joseph, protector of Holy Church, I ask your aid for the whole Church on earth, those who lead and serve her and all who look to her for guidance. With you as our example, help us to do God's work and enjoy the rewards He has promised. Amen.